ABOUT THE BOOK

This is the story of just one day in young Abe's life. Already he possessed the qualities which were later to mark him for greatness.

Though no child of twelve can possibly see the opportunities ahead of him, he can learn and study and be ready for his chance. This is just what Abe Lincoln did.

Abe Lincoln's Birthday differs from the countless other books on Lincoln's life in that the author is able to bring to the story a knowledge of pioneer days handed down to her from her grandmother's stories.

Mrs. Hays' family lived in the same neighborhood as the Lincolns. All the factual material and the relationships of the members of the Lincoln family are authentic.

The story of *Abe Lincoln's Birthday* can best be stated in a quote from his own writings, "I will prepare myself and maybe my chance will come."

Other Books by Wilma Pitchford Hays

CHRISTMAS ON THE MAYFLOWER

PILGRIM THANKSGIVING

THE STORY OF VALENTINE

FREEDOM

THE FOURTH OF JULY RAID

EASTER FIRES

Abe Lincoln's Birthday

by Wilma Pitchford Hays

Illustrated *by* Peter Burchard

Coward, McCann & Geoghegan, Inc. New York

©1961 by Wilma Pitchford Hays

All rights reserved. This book, or parts thereof, may not be reproduced in any form without permission in writing from the Publishers. Published simultaneously in the Dominion of Canada by Longmans, Green & Company, Toronto.

Library of Congress Catalog Card Number: 61-5886

Manufactured in the United States of America

Eighth Impression
SBN: GB 698-30001-7

To my grandmother, Susan Rebecca, and my father, her son, who told me stories of early pioneer days

Abe Lincoln waked in the cold dark, wide awake. He had heard a scratching on the roof of the cabin loft above his head. It sounded like the claws of an animal scrambling over the logs. Abe sat up and leaned on his elbow and long arms. His shock of thick black hair brushed the slanted roof as he listened for the scratching sound to come again.

There were no windows in the loft but Abe knew where there was a peephole. He and his older sister, Sarah, had helped their father build this cabin four years ago after they moved here to Indiana from Kentucky. Sarah and he had done most of the chinking.

In the back wall of the loft, they had found a wider-than-usual space between the logs. Abe had split wood into a thin slab and wedged it into the crack. Sarah dabbed it with wet clay, just as she was supposed to do. But before the clay dried, they had loosened the wedge so they could lift it from the crack when they wanted to see what was going on outside.

Carefully Abe drew his long legs from under the horsehide robe. He did not want to wake his stepbrother, John, or his cousin, Dennis, who slept beside him on the cornhusk mattress on the loft floor.

He knelt and pulled the wedge from the peephole. He pressed his cheek against the split logs and peered out into the bright moonlight on the snow. He could not see the roof of the cabin, but he could see the big oak tree that overhung the roof. Swinging on a rope from the tree was a quarter of venison which his father had hung to freeze, to supply their winter's meat when it was too stormy to hunt.

The frozen deermeat was swaying although there was no wind. Abe knew that the tree branch would not sway unless a large animal had been on it a few minutes before.

Probably a big wildcat, he thought. When the wildcat could not get at the meat from the tree branch, it must have jumped down on the roof and tried to leap at the meat from below.

Abe heard their four horses which were huddled for warmth close to the haystack behind the cabin. The horses were stomping and snorting. He felt even more sure that he had heard a wildcat on the roof.

Abe grinned. Wildcats were smart but his father was smarter. Tom Lincoln had built a little platform on the tree branch above the meat to prevent a wildcat from dropping down onto the venison. And he had hung the meat too high above the roof for the best leap a wildcat could make.

"I'll bet that was the wildest wildcat in Perry County, when it had to leave here without that meat," he said to himself.

Shivering he crawled back into bed without waking John or Dennis and pulled the horsehide robe up under his chin. Almost at once he heard a scratching sound again. He smiled and waited.

He knew that this soft scratching was made by their pet cat climbing the peg ladder to the loft. Puss had heard Abe moving about and was coming to investigate. It was funny how Puss could climb the rough wall to get into bed with him, but she would never go back down the wall by herself. He always had to carry her down on his shoulder.

Abe felt the cat whisker his cheek as she sniffed to be sure that it was Abe she had found in the dark. He lifted an arm and made a little cave under

the covers by his side. Puss crawled in, sweeping his face with her tail as she turned around and settled down with her chin over his arm.

"How am I going to sleep with you teakettling along like that?" he asked Puss.

She went on purring. Abe wasn't sleepy anyway now. He began to think of that time more than a year ago when his father had brought the kitten home to Sarah from one of the neighbors. Abe's lower lip pushed out, the way it always did when he was thinking hardest.

He hoped he would never know another time as sad and lonely as that winter had been right after his mother died. The fall had started out better than usual, too.

His mother's Aunt Betsy and Uncle Tom Sparrow had come from their old home in Kentucky to settle near the Lincolns. With them was Dennis Hanks, a cousin they had adopted. Dennis was seven years older than Abe and he teased Abe a lot about always having his nose in a book. But Dennis and Aunt Betsy and Uncle Tom were good company.

In the evenings they would come and sit around the fireplace in the Lincolns' cabin. They would swap true-story yarns about the days right after the Revolutionary War when their kinfolk had come with Dan'l Boone to settle Kentucky.

Abe had been named for his grandfather, Abraham Lincoln, captain of a Virginia Militia in the Revolution, and friend of Daniel Boone. His grandfather had been killed by Indians while he worked in his field with his small son, Tom, who had grown up to be Abe's father. Tom Lincoln often told this story.

Sometimes, when they were not swapping family stories, they read aloud to each other, stories from the Bible or from Aesop's *Fables*. Abe had read Aesop's *Fables* so many times that he knew most of them by heart. He liked to think about them and what they meant. It was hard to believe that a slave had written the fables; the Greek Aesop, captured by the Romans and made a slave. A pretty smart slave, Abe thought.

While the cat purred beneath his ear, Abe thought of how pleasant life had been that fall when his mother's aunt and uncle and Dennis Hanks were living in the half-cabin on his father's place until they could build their own home. The corn crop had been pretty good. He and his father continued to chop down trees and clear more land for more corn.

Abe had always been big for his age and he had been given an ax before he was eight. He had been swinging an ax nearly every day since then, four years—for today was February twelfth and he was twelve years old.

Abe wondered whether anyone in the family would remember that today was his birthday. Surely his sister would remember, since her birthday had been only two days before and she had had a skillet cake. But a girl needed more attention and comforting than a boy.

At least that was what Abe and his father had thought when Sarah cried so much after their mother, Nancy, died.

That fall his mother's aunt and uncle had begun to tremble with the dread milk-sick. No one knew what the cows sometimes ate to poison their milk, but everyone knew that few people recovered from the milk-sick. Abe's mother, Nancy, who had gray-blue eyes and thick black hair, and was healthy and slim and tall for a woman, took her aunt and uncle to her own cabin and nursed them until they died.

Five days later Nancy Lincoln took the milk-sick.

Abe remembered just what his mother had said to him when she called him to her bed. "I am going away from you, Abe. I know you'll be a good boy. Be kind to Sarah and your father. I want you to live as I have taught you and to love your Heavenly Father."

Abe tried not to think of that first year after his mother's death. Although his own heart was heavy, he knew it was hardest on Sarah. She had to work in the cabin alone while he and Dennis and his father worked in the fields and woods.

Dennis and Abe had brought pets to Sarah whenever they could catch a wild creature. Once they brought her a baby coon and once a little turtle, but both ran away. Then their father brought home the kitten, which Abe loved as much as Sarah did.

Then a little more than a year after his mother's death, his father had made ready for a trip back to their old home in Kentucky, a hundred miles away. He told Sarah and Abe why he was going.

"Do you remember the Johnson family who

lived near us in Elizabethtown?" Tom Lincoln asked his children.

Sarah and Abe nodded. "Elizabeth Johnson was my age," Sarah said, "and her brother, John, was younger than Abe."

"And there was a little sister named Matilda," Abe said, "and their father was dead."

Sarah and his father looked at Abe in surprise. "How you remember, Abe!" Sarah cried. "I'd forgotten there was a younger girl."

"Now, you need a mother and the Johnson children need a father," Tom Lincoln said. "I'm going to ask Sally Bush Johnson to marry me. I've known her a long time and she and your mother were friends. If she will have me, I will be gone several weeks. There'll be work to do there—packing their things to bring back with us, and all.

"I've laid in plenty of food for Sarah to cook. Abe, you and Dennis keep the wood chopped and milk the cow regular."

His father had taken the four horses and ridden away.

Abe had not known what to think about another woman coming to this cabin, using his mother's fry pans and Dutch oven, sitting in his mother's place at the puncheon table. He knew that his sister had not been able to cook as well as their mother had. She couldn't keep the cabin as clean, and their clothes all needed mending.

But another woman here. She might be bossy, or unkind. She might think that a boy, not quite eleven, should not be allowed to stay up at night and read by the firelight. Yet night was the only uninterrupted time he had to read.

Abe was worried, then he grew more cheerful. Mrs. Johnson might not want to leave Elizabethtown to live in the wilderness. She might not return with his father.

Then one December evening just before sundown, Abe and Sarah heard wagon wheels creaking and their father whistling. They ran from the cabin and stopped short to watch horses slowly drawing a wagon up the slope. Beside it, Tom Lincoln rode his favorite saddle horse, Old Vesta.

On the wagon seat sat a woman and two girls and a boy. A mountain of furniture and bundles of clothing and bedding were piled on the wagon bed.

Suddenly shy, Sarah and Abe backed against the cabin doorway. As the wagon pulled to a stop in front of them, Abe saw a real bureau, a set of chairs and a clothespress, featherbeds and pillows and a stack of kitchenware.

Sarah ran to greet her father and the Johnson children, who jumped from the wagon. The woman came and stood before Abe. She was as tall as his own mother but fair-skinned and she wore her hair curled.

She looked at Abe and he looked at her, and something very curious happened. Abe knew that he liked this woman, stepmother or not, and that she liked him. It was even more than liking, it was instant understanding of each other.

"I brought you some books, Abe," she said. "I recollect how you were always reading even when you were so young before you left Kentucky."

He liked her voice, so calm and friendly, and she had been his mother's friend.

"I used to tell Nancy," she continued, "that I never saw a boy who learned as fast as you. She always said, 'Yes, my boy will get on. He'll make a smart man of himself some day.'"

Abe smiled then and his new mother smiled. They had been close friends ever since. Even the next day when she suggested that he wash his mop of black hair and soap well behind his ears, something he hadn't bothered to do often that winter, Abe didn't mind.

She even understood the times when Abe had to be alone. She seemed to know that it was important, sometimes, for him to be quiet to read or just to think.

Once he had heard her say to his father, "Abe works good most of the time and he never gives us any trouble. When his mind is way-off-yonder like that, he's only trying to figure something out. Let him be. He'll get over it and be laughing and joking again soon enough."

Abe loved and missed his own mother very much. But he knew he was lucky to have a second mother like his. As far as that, his father was proud of Abe's book learning, too, except when it kept Abe from getting his work done.

Puss interrupted Abe's thoughts. She stretched and crawled out from under the covers and stood on his chest. She began to knead the horsehide robe with her front claws as if she were trying to tell Abe that it was daylight. It was time to get up even if the loft was still dark.

Sure enough, Abe heard his father moving about in the room below. His father heaped logs in the fireplace and blew on the coals until the fire was roaring. Then he went outdoors to milk the cow.

The three girls left their corner bed and ran to dress in front of the fire, shivering and giggling. In a few minutes his mother called, "All right, Abe! Dennis! John! Time to come down now."

Abe pulled on his linsey-woolsey shirt and buckskin breeches and moccasins. With Puss clinging to his shoulder, he backed down the peg ladder.

When all eight members of the family were seated for breakfast around the puncheon table, eating corn-meal mush with maple sugar, Abe said, "I think a wildcat was after our meat again. I heard something on the roof early this morning."

"Yes," his father said. "I saw its tracks in the snow. It's a big one."

"A panther is mighty dangerous," Dennis said.

Lots of people called wildcats panthers. By any name, a big tawny wildcat was something no one wanted to meet face to face.

"I recollect," Dennis said, "a panther clawed a boy real bad on Little Pigeon Creek last year."

The younger children stopped eating and looked at their father.

"That wildcat can't hurt you if you stay in the house when you hear it," Tom Lincoln said. "And there's no need for you to go outside if it comes. I hung that meat too high for the best leap the biggest wildcat can make." He pushed back his chair and stood up.

"Abe," he said, "you and I better get to work. I hear I'm to get the job of building the new Pigeon Creek church, so we must cut and trim as many building logs as we can this morning. At noon I have to go into town for a couple of days. I'm on jury duty—and I want to stop at an auction sale."

Abe remembered that his father had bought him a little homemade wagon once at an auction sale. His father had brought it home for his birthday when he was five. It didn't look as if anyone was going to remember that today was his twelfth birthday. Not that it mattered. He was getting pretty big to pay attention to birthdays.

Dennis left the table, too. He was going to help a new neighbor put up a cabin today.

Abe saw Dennis go to the corner cupboard and take down a jar of goose grease. That was funny. Abe hadn't noticed Dennis sniffling. Goose grease was for rubbing on the chest, throat, nose, and feet to cure a cold. His mother had roasted a goose for Christmas and skimmed off all the fat and stored it in jars to treat their winter colds.

Now Dennis was coming right toward Abe, and Dennis was grinning. Before Abe could duck or run, Dennis caught him around the shoulders and smeared his nose good with goose grease.

All the children laughed and shouted, "Happy birthday, Abe!"

Abe tried to wipe off the grease with his fingers. He might have known that Dennis would think "funning" was the best way to celebrate a birthday.

Dennis was laughing so hard that Abe finally grinned, too. At least they had remembered his

birthday. Then he saw that his father had left the cabin. Abe caught up his coonskin cap and jammed it on his head. He lifted his ax to his shoulder and followed Tom Lincoln.

His father was standing in the yard whistling for Old Vesta, the gray mare, who was eating hay stacked against the back of the cabin,

Vesta lifted her head, whinnied and trotted to meet Tom Lincoln. Abe saw his father stroke Vesta's mane and let her eat a chunk of maple sugar from his palm.

His father had brought his horses from Kentucky, where everyone was proud of their fine saddle and race horses.

Old Vesta could no longer run very fast but she was still proud and smart. She was like one of the family.

Abe and his father walked beside Vesta to the woods. About the only time Abe felt boy-sized was when he was with his six-foot, two-hundred-pound father with his shock of black hair and weather-browned skin.

All morning his father cut and felled trees. Abe trimmed the branches of each tree close to the trunk to make a first-rate building log. Then he fastened a chain around the log and hitched it to Old Vesta who pulled the log to the open hillside to dry.

There was little time for talking while they worked, although his father whistled often and sometimes sang.

"Go tell Aunt Rhoady, go tell Aunt Rhoady,
  Go tell Aunt Rhoady, her old gray goose is dead.
The one she's been saving, the one she's been
    saving,
The one she's been saving to make a feather-bed!"

His father was usually good-natured. On days when they did something quiet, like mending harness, his father told jokes and stories. Abe liked to work with his father. He remembered many of the jokes to tell later to his friends.

After a noon snack of corn-bread dodgers and fried pork, his father said, "Abe, your mother

needs corn meal. You'll have to go to the mill this afternoon."

Abe liked to go to the mill. Sometimes he saw friends there, and he always took a book to read while the corn was being ground.

"Take that sack of corn hanging in the loft," his father continued. "You can ride Old Vesta, but get a move on and get back before dark." Then his father rode off on the stallion for jury duty in the town.

Abe found Old Vesta standing in a clump of sassafras bushes. She was nibbling at the bare twigs and bark as if they tasted better than the dried winter hay. Abe whistled to her but she didn't come. Maybe she thought she had worked enough for one day. Abe knew that Vesta had a mind of her own all right.

He walked across the clearing to the sassafras bushes, whistling and talking to Vesta as he had heard his father do. She pricked up her ears and watched him as if she meant to run if he came closer. He reached out his hand, palm up with a chunk of maple sugar in it.

That changed her mind. Vesta trotted to him and lifted the sugar with her soft upper lip.

Abe slipped the bridle on her and jumped onto her back.

The mill was a couple of miles away. Abe rode along the narrow wagon trail lined with trees and underbrush on each side. He had helped his father cut this trail through "roughs" when they came to Indiana. He would never forget how slowly they had moved with their horses and wagon from Thompson's Ferry to their homesite. They had cut their way through thickets and tangled grapevines, and they felled oak and hickory trees with their axes as they went.

Now Abe looked at the dead grapevines clinging to bare trees and wished he could find even a cluster of dried-up grapes hanging there. He was tired of eating corn-meal mush and corn bread and meat three times a day, every day.

He looked at his long thin legs and at Vesta's ribs showing under her gray hide. Men and animals alike were lean in late winter. Not that they were starving, but there was no doubt that winter eating was pretty slim pickings alongside summer eating.

In the summer his mother and the girls raised a good garden with all kinds of vegetables and melons. In summer he could stop and eat in the woods or fields most any place. He had found wild strawberries so thick that although he tried not to step on them, his bare feet were red with juice. And there were wild blackberries, red raspberries, persimmons, and pawpaw, plums and crab apples. In the fall the whole family went after hickory nuts and hazelnuts. Sometimes they found wild bees' honey in a hollow tree.

Abe grew hungry just thinking about all these good things which were months away yet.

Abe heard a rustle in the thicket. Vesta's ears pricked up and Abe thought of the wildcat. Then he saw a flash of green. He looked closer. From a tree a wild parakeet was watching him. The big bird, with yellow head and throat and a cap of orange-red, was so pretty that Abe felt cheered just to see it. It flew ahead of him from tree to tree and called in a shrill voice.

It is probably looking for food, too, Abe thought. Everything is hungry; but spring must be on its way if the first wild parrot has returned.

The passenger pigeons would be coming soon, now. A short distance from their cabin on Little Pigeon Creek was a passenger-pigeon roosting grounds. Abe had seen thousands of the wild gray and white pigeons fly over the cabin together, so thick they hid the sun as if they were clouds passing. Abe wouldn't hunt the pretty creatures but he had eaten them when his father or Dennis brought them home.

Abe reached the clearing where Noah Gordon had built a horse mill. Each customer must use his own horse. Abe saw that someone was there before him. He would have to wait his turn. He recognized the roan horse turning the mill. It belonged to a neighbor, Mr. Hall.

Abe slid off Vesta and lifted the sack of corn from her back. He slip-knotted her bridle reins to a hitching post. Then he took the rope from the sack of corn and tied the halter rope around Vesta's neck to secure her a second time.

Grinding corn with a horse hitched to a beam, the horse plodding round and round the well-beaten circle path, was slow business. Abe didn't know how long he would have to wait until Mr. Hall was through grinding his corn meal. And Vesta would stand just so long before she lost patience and slipped off her bridle and trotted home. Abe wasn't taking any chances of being left to walk two miles through the thicket in the early dark of winter.

Abe sat down on the frozen ground with his back against a tree. From inside his wool shirt he took a book, *Pilgrim's Progress*. He had wanted to bring a new book, borrowed from a neighbor, *The Life of George Wahington*. Abe had read it through only once, but he wouldn't risk carrying a borrowed book from the cabin.

His father had brought *Pilgrim's Progress* to Abe when he was nine years old. He remembered how his mother, Nancy, had helped him sound out many of the words that were strange to him then.

Abe and Sarah had gone to school a few months in Kentucky before they moved to Indiana. They'd

had a few weeks' schooling since, when the neighbors joined together to pay a teacher to hold a "subscription school" for their children. But teachers didn't stay long in the wilderness. Abe had taught himself by reading his books over and over.

While Abe found the place he wanted to read in the book, he thought of the choice the writer, John Bunyan, had had to make. John Bunyan could stay out of prison if only he would do what other people wanted him to do rather than what he believed to be right.

John Bunyan wrote that he had "been tossed for many weeks" by the temptation to stay with his family and not go to prison. Finally Bunyan knew that he must do what was right, no matter what happened to him. "I must do it," he had written. "I must do it."

Tears came into Abe's eyes just to think of that poor man parting from his wife and children and lingering in prison so many years.

It isn't likely, Abe thought, that when I grow up, I will ever have such a hard decision to make.

But if I ever do, I hope I can be as strong as John Bunyan and do what is right, no matter what happens to me.

"Howdy, Abe," his neighbor, Mr. Hall, said.

Abe looked up and blinked as if he were trying to remember just where he was.

Mr. Hall laughed. "I knew your mind was away yonder when I saw your lower lip pushed out," he said. "You got a habit pushing your lip out when you read or think hard."

Abe grinned and stood up and stretched the cramps from his long gangling legs. "Howdy, Mr. Hall," he said. "I see you have your corn ground."

Mr. Hall turned from lifting a sack of corn meal onto his roan horse. "Are you reading that *Robinson Crusoe* book again?" he asked.

"Not this time," Abe said.

"I like that story," Mr. Hall said. "That Crusoe feller had about as much trouble keeping alive on that island as we have here settling the wilderness."

Abe went to the log shelter that served as office for Noah Gordon, the millwright. Mr. Gordon

was not there. He had left an older boy, about sixteen, to tend the mill, a boy as tall as Abe and half again as heavy.

The mill tender took the share of corn which Abe gave him to pay for the use of the mill. He said, "I like my supper early, so get a move on."

Abe walked over to Vesta and untied her and

led her to the mill. He hitched her to the end of the beam which turned the machinery and grinding stone. Vesta pulled back and braced herself to show how much she disliked walking round and round without going any place, like some dumb ox.

Abe gave her a gentle slap on the rump. "Get along," he ordered. "We want to get home sometime tonight."

Vesta shook her head but she began to plod around the circular track. She made about a dozen turns, then she began to limp.

Abe stopped her. He lifted her left hind hoof and ran his finger around the groove inside her iron shoe. There was no pebble there and her shoe wasn't loose.

He gave Vesta another pat and sent her on her way. She limped more and more. Abe knew better than to allow a horse to work if there was anything wrong with her hoof. She could be lamed for good and become useless.

Abe examined her hoof even more carefully.

He couldn't find a thing wrong. The mill tender came and looked at the hoof too.

"What's wrong with that horse?" he asked sourly. "Get her moving. I want to close up here."

Suddenly Abe laughed. There was nothing wrong. That Vesta was up to tricks again.

"Vesta may be getting old," Abe said to the mill tender, "but she's smart enough to know what she does *not* like to do. She's just playing lame."

"You mean that horse is only *acting* like her hoof hurts?" the big boy growled.

Abe was still laughing. "She thinks I'll quit and take her home," he said.

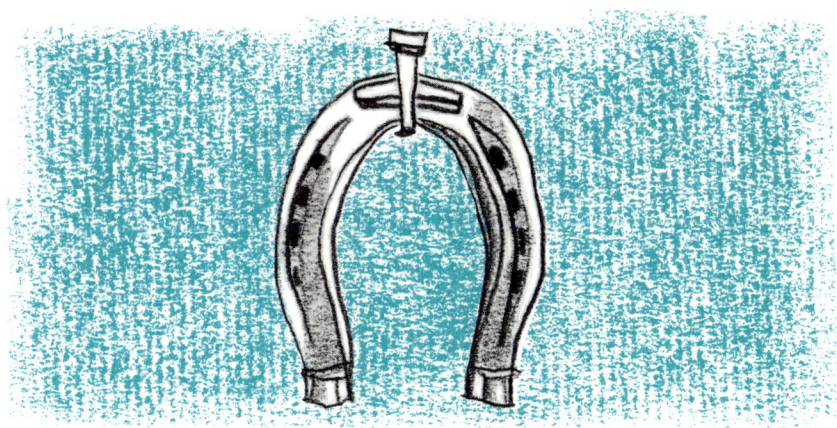

Before Abe realized what was happening, the mill tender caught up a club of wood and struck Vesta across the rump. The horse leaped forward and whinnied.

Abe felt heat prickle up his jaws and into his hair.

"I'll teach that horse to play tricks," the big boy shouted and raised the club to strike again,

Abe moved quickly and caught the mill tender's wrist in his long fingers. The bigger boy tried to twist loose from Abe's grip, but Abe's muscles were strong from swinging an ax every day. He squeezed the older boy's wrist until he was forced to drop the club.

"You better know more than the horse does— before you try to teach her anything," Abe said.

The mill tender drew back his fist, then seemed to think better of hitting Abe. He stood rubbing his wrist.

Abe wasn't looking for a fight if the other fellow wasn't. He turned to Vesta.

She was trembling, her ears laid back. Abe

clucked to her soothingly. He took her rein and led her around the track. She was so jumpy from the surprise of being hit that Abe continued to walk with her until the corn was ground into meal. As long as Abe went with her, Vesta never limped again, then, or on their way home.

It was dusk when Abe stopped before the cabin. He saw that Dennis had not yet returned from the cabin-raising at the neighbors, for his horse wasn't here. Abe lifted the sack of corn meal from Vesta's back and dropped it beside the door. While he curried the snow and mud balls from Vesta's hoofs, Puss came to meet him. She wound in and out between his long legs, arching and purring, until Abe almost tripped over her.

When Abe carried the sack of meal into the cabin, supper was ready. On the puncheon table he saw corn-meal bread and venison. He dipped his hands into the gourd of soft soap hanging above the washstand beside the door, and washed his hands and face.

His mother came to him and said, "Your father

got up on the roof and cut the steaks from the frozen deer quarter early this morning. He wanted you to have venison for your birthday, Abe."

"It looks real good," Abe said. He didn't need to tell her how he craved an apple or even a mess of pigweed greens.

"I wanted to make you a skillet cake," she said, "but I used the last wheat flour for Sarah's. Your father plans to bring you a present of newspapers when he comes back, though."

They had almost finished eating when they heard a heavy thump on the roof, and an angry snarl. The wildcat had come back and leaped and missed the meat.

Sarah and Elizabeth and Matilda, sitting side by side across the table from Abe, hunched closer together. John, at the end near his mother, swallowed and looked at Abe.

"The wildcat can't hurt us as long as we are in here—and it is out there," Abe said. "It will give up after a while and go away."

They listened to the wildcat pacing back and

forth on the roof. No one wanted any more to eat. Abe left the table and moved over in front of the fireplace,

Then they heard a loud crying, the way a kitten cries when it has gone too high into a tree and turned about and is afraid to come down.

"That's Puss," Sarah cried. "Oh, Abe, what will happen to Puss?"

"She'll have to stay up in the tree until the wildcat leaves," Abe said.

"How do you know the wildcat isn't after Puss?" Sarah cried.

Abe frowned. He couldn't be sure, not the way Puss was yowling and spitting. Puss gave an awful cry. Abe ran and threw open the door.

The night was black. He couldn't see a thing. But from the sounds, there was no doubt that Puss was high in the tree where the meat was hung. She must have scampered up there when the wildcat came.

Puss continued to spit and hiss, but Abe could hear no more from the roof. Maybe the wildcat had gone.

Abe took one step into the dark and turned to look up at the roof. For a moment he couldn't move. Directly over him, above the doorway, glowed two large green eyes. Abe couldn't see whether or not the wildcat was crouched to spring, and he didn't wait to find out.

He leaped back into the cabin and shut the door after him. Puss yowled even louder, pleading for rescue.

Finally Abe couldn't bear to listen to her yowls any longer. He caught up the unburned end of a stick of wood from the fire. The other end smoked and blazed into a torch as he opened the door.

"Don't go, Abe," Sarah cried.

"Be careful," his mother called.

The others seemed too frightened or fascinated to speak.

Abe brandished the flames in front of him. He shouted and made a great racket.

The wildcat snarled and stood its ground. The hungry animal wasn't going to be driven from the food it hoped to get.

Abe swung the blazing firewood as near the

roof as he dared. The big cat snarled and ran up on the roof ridge and turned its green eyes on Abe again. Abe hesitated, wondering if he could make it back into the cabin before the wildcat leaped on him.

Then, with a last snarl, the big cat ran along the ridge and leaped off the back of the cabin. Abe heard the horses snort and stomp. Seconds later, the wildcat screamed once from the edge of the clearing as it entered the woods, an angry cry that sounded almost like a woman's scream.

Abe placed the torch on the ground so that its fire wouldn't frighten Puss. He went to the oak tree and coaxed her down the trunk to a limb where he could reach her. He scooped her up and carried her into the cabin.

While everyone was gathered around Puss to pet and console her, Dennis came home. There were so many talking at once that Dennis couldn't get the story straight at first. Finally he realized what had happened.

"You mean you let that panther get away,

Abe?" he said. "Why didn't you grab Tom's gun and shoot it?"

"Because," Abe said, "I was more scared of that wildcat than it was of me."

When the excitement was over and the girls were washing dishes, they asked Abe to tell them stories. Sarah and Elizabeth wanted to hear the fable about the Wind and the Sun. John wanted to hear about the boy who called "Wolf, wolf" falsely so many times that when a wolf really came and he needed help, no one came to his rescue.

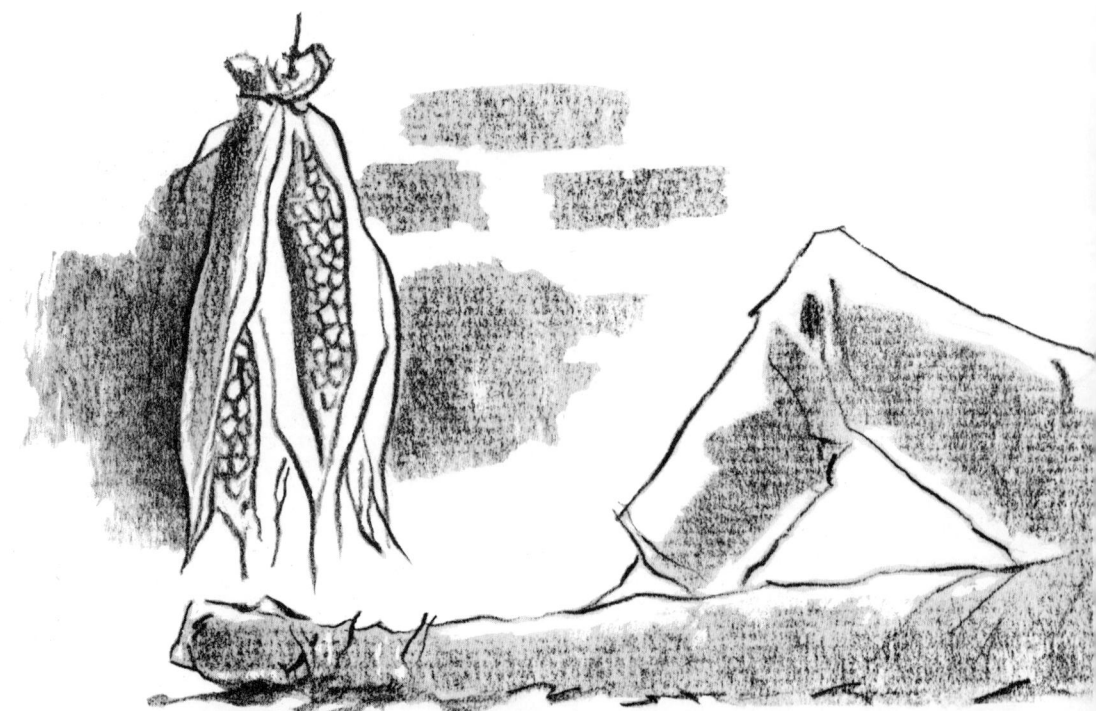

"Abe," Dennis said, "tell us the yarn about the feller that sailed the flatboat up to the rock and the rock was magnetized and drawed all the nails right out of his boat, and he got a duckin'."

Abe laughed. "From the *Arabian Nights*," he said. "Well, I'll tell that, too."

He stretched out on the bearskin in front of the fire and told their favorite stories from memory almost word for word as he had read them so many times in his books. Abe liked to tell a story almost as much as he liked to read. That way he caught

the idea twice, through his eyes as he read and through his ears as he heard himself repeat it.

When he had finished telling the stories, Abe was tired. But at night, when the cabin was quiet, was his best time to read. He took from the top of the corner cupboard his borrowed book, *The Life of George Washington.*

Dennis, following John up the peg ladder to their bed in the loft, paused and looked over his shoulder. "What you reading?" he asked.

"About the first President of the United States," Abe answered.

"You figure on learning *how* to be President?" Dennis teased.

"Maybe," Abe said and sat down on the bearskin rug.

Dennis grinned widely. "Folks want a President to look important, Abe—and you're just *too much legs* to be handsome."

Abe turned over on his stomach. By the light from the fire he began to read about George

Washington, the father of his country. Behind him, Abe heard the three girls go to their bed in a far corner of the room. His mother went to her bed in the opposite corner.

Then for a long time there was no sound except the crackle of the fire, the turning of the leaves of his book, the occasional stretch and yawn of Puss curled beside him on the bearskin, and the stomp of the horses' hoofs outside as they huddled against the cabin for protection from the winter winds.

After a long time he heard Sarah whisper, "Abe?"

"Yes," he mumbled and went on reading.

His sister came with a shawl wrapped around her and sat on the bearskin beside him. "Abe," she said," did you mean what you said to Dennis?"

"What did I say?"

"About maybe being President some day."

He smiled. "Me, President! I was just funning."

"Remember when you were little?" Sarah

asked. "You used to climb on a chair and make speeches to Mother while she worked about the cabin."

Abe remembered all right. He remembered how his real mother used to listen and smile.

"Mother used to say," Sarah went on, "that you were bound to become a preacher when you grew up—the way you could spout off everything you heard anyone say."

"I want more than talking now," Abe said. He closed his book on his finger. "Sarah, did you ever want something?" he asked. "Want it *real* bad, I mean?"

"Not real bad," she said slowly.

"I want time to read—and read—and read," he said. "I want to know a lot more than how to swing an ax, and grub out stumps, and hoe corn. And most of what I want to learn is in books, if I can read enough of them.

"Even some of my best friends are in books, Sarah. I think I'd know John Bunyan and Robinson Crusoe if I met them on the trail. And what wouldn't I give to meet George Washington! Did

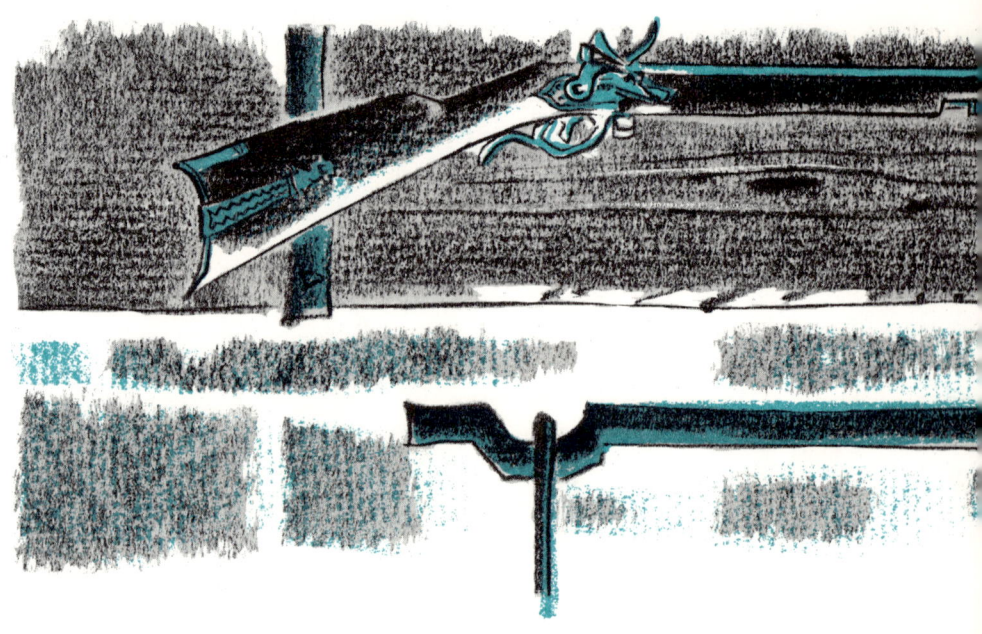

you know that George Washington could out-wrestle and outrun about anyone when he was young?"

"*That's* like you, Abe," Sarah said.

"And listen to this," Abe said in a low voice that wouldn't wake the sleeping family.

Sarah waited while he tried to find the page he wanted to read aloud.

"Here it is," he said. "George Washington and his soldiers are ready to cross the river to fight the Battle of Trenton in the Revolutionary War. Gen-

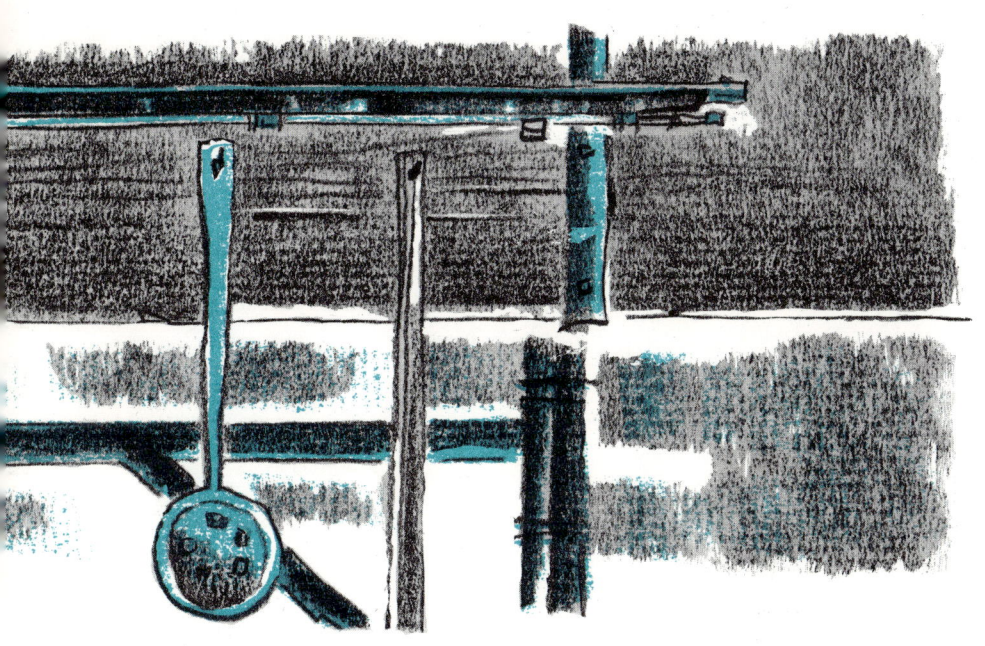

eral Washington knows his supplies are short. His men are ragged and starving. Some of them have marched barefoot through the snow to this riverbank."

Abe looked down at his book. As he read, he felt as if he were right there with General Washington and his men on that dark night. Along with them, Abe could feel the pelting hail and the sting of snow blinding his eyes. He seemed to be standing with the soldiers on the riverbank, hearing the roar of the flood. He felt the fearful danger of crossing the angry waters to face the enemy in their camps. He seemed to see George Washington ride before his troops with sword upraised.

He heard General Washington's voice as he called to his soldiers, "Take courage, men. Remember what you fight for!"

Abe closed the book. He was so stirred that it was a long moment before he could speak.

"These men must have been struggling for something most important," he said to Sarah, "even more important than National Independence. I think each man wanted to be free himself. And he wanted to hold out a promise to all people in the world to be free—for all time to come. That's why these men fought, and that's why they formed a union of the states to protect their liberty."

Abe fell silent, thinking. Sarah stood up and started back to bed. Then she turned to her brother again.

"Abe," she said, "you're honest and strong. You'd be like these men if you ever have to fight for what is right."

Abe rolled over and looked into the fire. Sarah believed that he could do anything he wanted to do. His real mother had been proud of his longing to learn, and his new mother encouraged him. But he knew that he was a long way from being somebody. He didn't even know for sure what he wanted to be when he grew up.

He pushed his lower lip out to help him think. No one, on his twelfth birthday, can know what he will become some day, Abe decided. The best thing I can do is to study and prepare myself—and maybe my chance will come.

The Author says:

The people in this story are real. From historical records, we know their real names and personalities, what the Lincoln family cabin was like, what they ate and where they slept. (The first winter after the Lincolns moved from Kentucky to Indiana, when Abe was almost eight years old, they lived in a dirt-floored half-cabin put up hastily to shelter them while they built the better cabin which is their home in this story. They were living in the new cabin when Nancy Hanks Lincoln died of the milk-sick, caused by the cows eating poison snakeroot plant.)

From Lincoln's own later writings and from the memories of people who knew him, we know the books Abe Lincoln read when he was a boy and some of the things Abe thought and said when he read them. We even know that Abe loved cats and that his family owned four horses when they moved from Kentucky to Indiana.

And all the world knows that Abraham Lincoln taught himself to be a lawyer, a great speaker and writer, and became a President of the United States. His name is linked in history with his hero, George Washington. Men said, "Washington was the father of his country, Lincoln was its savior."

In addition to the historical and factual background, I was able to add my own ancestors' reports of pioneer life in Kentucky, Indiana and Missouri. Three of my father's kinsmen were pioneers in Hardin County, Kentucky when Thomas and Nancy Lincoln lived there.

When I was a girl, my grandmother used to tell me stories of these early days, stories which *her* grandmother had told her. She told me about hanging the winter's meat in trees to freeze and how wildcats attempted to steal it, and of goose grease used to cure colds, and about their smart Kentucky horses.

Abraham Lincoln's family was typical of these pioneers, most of whom were descendants of Revolutionary War veterans who followed Daniel Boone to Kentucky and settled there. Later the

Lincoln family moved west to Indiana, and finally Illinois, where Abe was living when he was elected President of the United States.

W. P. H.

DATE DUE			
2-20			
SEP 1 2 1975			
MAY 11 '78			
OCT 12 '77			
APR 28 '78			
SEP 14 '78			
SEP 16 '79			
NOV 8 '79			
DEC 10 '80			
MAY 7 '84			
FEB 14 '85			
FEB 19 '91			
FEB 2 4 1994			

IDEAL 3370 UNGUMMED, 3371 GUMMED   PRINTED IN U.S.A.